GROWTH
MINDSET
book

By Barry Hymer &
Mike Gershon

Cartoons:
Phil Hailstone

Published by:

Teachers' Pocketbooks
Laurel House, Station Approach,
Alresford, Hampshire SO24 9JH, UK
Tel: +44 (0)1962 735573
Fax: +44 (0)1962 733637
Email: sales@teacherspocketbooks.co.uk
Website: www.teacherspocketbooks.co.uk

*Teachers' Pocketbooks is an imprint of
Management Pocketbooks Ltd.*

Series editor – Linda Edge

© Barry Hymer & Mike Gershon 2014

This edition published 2014. Reprinted 2015.
ISBN 978 1 906610 60 9

E-book ISBN 978 1 908284 72 3

British Library Cataloguing-in-Publication Data
– A catalogue record for this book is available
from the British Library.

Design, artwork and graphics by **Efex Ltd**.
Printed in UK.

Contents

Foreword from Carol Dweck

"I am delighted to recommend this important book. The authors explain my research on students' motivation and mindset elegantly and succinctly, and show how it can be applied in everyday learning and teaching. With research evidence, classroom examples, and case histories, they show how developing a growth mindset in students can be transformational.

The *Growth Mindset Pocketbook* has the potential to have a lasting impact on the lives of teachers and learners alike."

Carol S. Dweck, Author of Mindset: *How We Can Fulfil Our Potential*, Lewis & Virginia Eaton Professor of Psychology, Stanford University

Welcome

Thank you for buying this book. Whilst there is no one golden bullet in education (not even synthetic phonics), there is an approach that:

- Is underpinned by forty years of internationally-recognised research
- Is fundamentally relevant to your daily practice, and in all phases of education
- Transfers benefits across subject domains, and between home and school
- Supports learners to take control of their own learning
- Raises your own and your pupils' aspirations

Welcome

- Gets pupils embracing tough challenges
- Nurtures intrinsic motivation, as well as the skills of collaboration
- Promotes steady progress and high levels of scholastic achievement
- Underpins high levels of achievement beyond the school years, into work or higher education
- Is free to implement

Does this seem too good to be true? This book sets out to show how these benefits might begin to be seen in your classroom, this year. Please put it to the test.

Barry & Mike

The Nature of Mindset

What are mindsets?

What makes you *you*? Your mind? Your genes? Your experiences? Your irresistible personality or your stunning good looks? OK, you'll need more than a dip into a Pocketbook to crack that one, so let's try a variant: whatever makes you you, can you affect it? Your answer gives us a glimpse into your **mindset**. A mindset is simply a belief – a belief about yourself and your most fundamental qualities like ability, faith (or lack of it), personality, political views, talents, etc.

People with **fixed mindsets** believe that fundamental qualities like intelligence are essentially stable: they don't change much over time. People with **growth mindsets** believe that these qualities are, well, growable: they are susceptible to change and can flourish in certain circumstances and wither in others.

Two further questions:
* Does it really matter what mindset you have?
* Are mindsets changeable?

That's the whole point of this book. In brief, yes and yes. Mindsets really, really matter.

Beliefs vs ability

How many of these terms and expressions have you heard, or used?:

God-given talent   Innate gifts   Effortless success   Tone deaf

Like father, like son   Genetically gifted   Certain to do well

Natural athlete   Perfect pitch   Genius will out

They all seem to locate performance within the Victorian notion of genetic inheritance and pre-existent ability. Despite their continued prevalence, this century has seen an explosion of evidence that there are many better predictors of performance success than such fuzzy *capacity* concepts as intelligence, ability, talent, etc. **Persistence**, for instance – sheer grit.

What seems to matter is not your ability, but your beliefs about your ability. Do you believe it's something you can develop, or does it define your past, present and future?

What ability *per se* has contributed to humanity

Earlier, we named intelligence as an example of one of your *fundamental qualities*. The curious thing is, it's a whole lot *less* fundamental than the Western world seems to believe. We could summarise the contribution of ability alone to the march of civilisation as:

Zilch.
Nuffink.
Diddly squat.

The evidence base

So where's the evidence for the extraordinary claim that ability itself never solved, created or invented anything? Just look at the detailed and corroborated biographies and autobiographies of *any* influential problem-solver, creator and inventor through the ages: ability triumphs *only* in tandem with **opportunity, motivation** and **volition** – actually *creating* ability in the process. That includes Mozart, Marie Curie and Katie Price.

What's more, genome-mappers and other scientists have failed so far to locate any 'gifted' gene or the existence of a truly talented zygote.

And what about the claim that what people *believe* about their ability has a highly significant influence on their *actual* achievement? There are many studies in psychology that support this claim, but the person who has done most to substantiate it is the Stanford University academic, Professor Carol Dweck* – the originator of mindset theory.

*Carol Dweck's book *Self Theories* is still the best summary of her research.

The evidence base

Over four decades and countless studies, Carol Dweck and other mindset researchers have provided empirical evidence that people with growth mindsets are more:

- Open to challenges and constructively critical feedback
- Resilient in the face of obstacles and initial failure
- Convinced that individual effort makes a difference
- Likely to attribute success and failure to their own efforts, rather than to their innate abilities
- Able to learn well with and from others
- Likely to rise to the top – and stay there

And people with growth mindsets are *less* likely to cheat. There's no need: a poor performance is no reflection on their intelligence – it's simply an indication that they need to work harder or differently at that particular skill.

Little wonder that Dweck's work underpins some of the most powerful learning interventions in schools today, including formative assessment practices, Habits of Mind (Art Costa), Building Learning Power (Guy Claxton), etc.

Why do mindsets matter?

Consider Rowan and Naz, two classmates of similar achievement levels and socio-economic background. You give them the same task. It's well-pitched, high-challenge, designed to stretch them, and loved by Ofsted (you've been on the training course!).

Rowan sets to with gusto. He's good at this sort of task and values his reputation as someone who gets things right, fast. He finds the task unusually tough and quickly becomes dispirited, worrying that he's coming across as 'slow'. He tells his classmates the task's 'boring' and he disengages from it.

Naz sets to with gusto. He finds the task tough and his intellectual arousal is heightened. His initial attempts lead nowhere and he laughs when he realizes he's going down a blind alley. He tries a new strategy and engages classmates in a task-focused discussion. He shows curiosity and tenacity and steadily makes progress.

From a comparable baseline, Naz's growth mindset will trump Rowan's fixed mindset, and these effects will become increasingly marked over time. Mindsets matter.

A mindset's effects

The reasons behind Rowan and Naz's very different responses to the same task can be inferred from the following table:

Mindset	Intelligence is fixed (eg Rowan)	Intelligence is growable (eg Naz)
Priority	Prove my learning (show I'm bright).	Improve my learning (become brighter).
Seeks out …	Quick wins, easy successes, less able competitors, as these all show that I'm intellectually well-endowed.	Challenges, smart friends and other opportunities to learn and improve, as these all assist my development.
Avoids …	Tough challenges, effort, difficulty, higher-performing peers.	Tasks and situations that I've already mastered – no new learning there then.
When things get tough …	I become flaky, flustered and flounder, or simply walk away from the task, doubting my capacity to accomplish it. Or maybe I'll cheat.	I try harder or revise my strategy. I show resilience, creativity and grit – and thereby become a better learner.

Don't most people have growth mindsets?

Surely growth mindsets are the default setting for most people? Well, no.
However much you personally believe that Naz's growth mindset is simply common
sense – 'Of course effort makes a difference!' – don't expect all your pupils (or indeed
all your colleagues!) to believe this.

Research studies suggest that about 40% of us have a fixed mindset and a similar
proportion have a growth mindset, and that these mindsets are fairly stable across
domains, be they sporting, artistic, academic, etc.

However, roughly 15-20% of people are undecided or have mixed mindsets – growth
in some domains and fixed in others. For example, I might believe that practice makes
perfect when it comes to learning to drive, but as for computers, I was born without
the Windows gene!

The statistics quoted relate to vast sample sizes – in any one class you might well find
higher proportions of one mindset over another.

Don't bright people have growth mindsets?

It isn't the case that bright people are more likely to have growth mindsets. Fixed and growth mindsets seem to be fairly evenly distributed across populations irrespective of such variables as race, gender, age, class and 'ability'. You're as likely to come across a pupil with a fixed mindset in a top academic set as in a lower set – but the effect of a bright pupil having a fixed mindset can be particularly pernicious (especially, it seems, for girls): if people invest deeply in their being 'highly intelligent' and see their intelligence as an explanation for high achievement, then challenges to their self-image in the form of setbacks, obstacles or failures will be very keenly felt.

Our hunch is you've already encountered this, in the form of your own Rowans – those bright pupils who *just have* to get things right, first time, and before anyone else – and who are existentially crushed when they don't.

A little caveat
Although bright pupils aren't more likely to have growth mindsets, people with growth mindsets do tend to become 'brighter' over time. They develop more effective learning skills and strategies, and become more aware of themselves as learners, not merely as performers.

Mindset's origins

Where do Rowan's and Naz's different mindsets come from? Three candidates:

	Fixed mindset	Growth mindset
1. Praise and other rewards	Rowan has always been praised for getting things right, and quickly – *'Clever boy!'* He now does things in measured proportion to the praise he receives.	Naz hasn't had much praise from his parents, but they do notice and comment on his hard work and show interest in his activities – *'So why did you choose this colour?'* They give helpful feedback.
2. Over-valuing 'self-esteem'	Rowan's parents are effusive about his every action. Why not? To be critical (or even neutral) would crush his fragile 'self-esteem'.	Naz's parents don't see it as their job to donate self-esteem. Instead they help him see problems as intrinsically interesting, and to value effort not easy success.
3. The 'hidden curriculum'	Rowan notices how interested his parents are in his performance relative to his peers'. Labels like *'clever'*, *'stupid'*, *'quick'*, *'slow'* are used to describe people.	Naz notices how his parents value the effort and dedication that go into people's achievements, and how seldom people are described in terms of their *'natural abilities'*.

The role of parents

So are parents to blame for children's fixed mindsets? In part, yes, but few of us set out consciously to create non-learning offspring, and we're the products of our own upbringing and society's influences. Consider this (abridged) letter to an agony aunt*:

My son of eight is doing badly at school. I know he's clever, but he just can't be bothered. He's so lazy ... His teachers are getting fed up too. ... He can do the work, it's just that he won't. Is there anything we can do?

Alongside some very reasonable and perceptive comments (especially given the wider context of the letter), the response also included some advice that was well-intentioned but deeply misguided, eg:

Tell your son that he's clever .... Look at his homework with him and praise him to the skies when he gets the right answers. Take his side against the 'idiot teachers' who are scolding him .... Find out if it might not be a good idea if he's moved from his class – either up or down .... Sometimes, particularly with people who are basically bright, confidence can make them brighter.

*Virginia Ironside's Dilemmas. The Independent, 2nd November 2009

Good advice for parents

The evidence suggests a very different response would be appropriate. Based on forty years of research into motivation and pupil achievement, something along these lines would have been excellent advice for the concerned parent:

Leave off this 'clever' stuff! Whatever you do, **don't** say things like, 'You should find this easy – you're a bright boy!' Look at his homework with him, and show interest in it. Express delight when you find things puzzling and challenging: 'Wow – this is tough – we should learn something useful here!' When the task is easy, express mild disappointment and find ways to make things more interesting. Talk to his teachers and see if they can personalise the work sometimes. If he can do the work already, could they relate the homework to a real-life project or problem, and/or get him to do it jointly with a good friend? Go easy on the praise, stickers and rewards, but don't stint on the feedback or interest in his activity. Look to a change of class or school only as a last resort.

The dangers of 'being clever'

So just what's wrong with being clever, and being told that you're clever?

Nothing's wrong with being clever. Becoming clever is the very point of education after all – at least in the sense of becoming a skilled, knowledgeable and effective learner. But reassuring children that they *are* clever – whether they are or not – serves to (mis)direct children away from the task at hand (immersion in the process of learning) and towards an obsession with their success or failure (and flawed explanations for the performance product).

So praising them for their intelligence inadvertently leads to the sort of brittle intellectual self-confidence that shatters in the face of 'failure':

> If my smartness explains my successes, then my lack of smartness must explain my failures. So how can I best protect my self-image from threat? By choosing tasks and activities that doom me to easy success, and by avoiding tough challenges at all costs.

Fixed mindsets can be safe and comfortable, but they lead nowhere.

The dangers of 'not being clever'

What about constantly being told you're clever when actually you're only averagely clever, or maybe not that clever at all?

A focus on the concept of intelligence has the same terrible effect, regardless of where you fall on the ability spectrum. There are many inadvertent victims of caring adults' attempts to boost a person's confidence and self-esteem in just this way. These are people who either end up with little self-awareness (check the early rounds of *The X-Factor*), or who end up with a sense of never achieving as a 'clever' person might be expected to achieve, who are terrified of exams or other measures of their 'fixed ability', who have zero confidence or resilience, few strategies in their learning toolkits and certainly no growth mindset.

Are mindsets measurable?

Mindsets are observable – you'll see them expressed as learning or non-learning behaviours: Naz's dogged persistence, for instance, contrasted with Rowan's anxious defensiveness. But for many years Carol Dweck has also found a simple but surprisingly effective way of measuring people's mindsets for research purposes.

Children aged ten and over are asked to read each sentence below and to circle the one number that shows how much they agree with it, according to this key. (They are told there are no 'wrong' or 'right' answers.)

You have a certain amount of intelligence and you really can't do much to change it.	1	2	③	4	5	6
Your intelligence is something about you that you can't change very much.	①	2	3	4	5	6
You can learn new things, but you can't really change your basic intelligence.	1	②	3	4	5	6

1. Strongly agree   2. Agree   3. Mostly agree   4. Mostly disagree   5. Disagree   6. Strongly disagree

Try measuring

You could try the same questions on your own pupils. From their responses to these three questions, calculate an average score for each pupil. An average score of 1-3 suggests a strongly or mildly fixed mindset, and 4-6 suggests a mildly or strongly growth mindset.

Tally up the number of pupils scoring 1-3 and those scoring 4-6. These are potentially useful general indicators of **a class's mindset** – ie the proportion of fixed and growth mindset learners in the class as a whole – but reliability for individuals is relatively low.

How about you? Respond with a ruthless honesty. If your average score was 6, you're probably a tiger-teacher with a rampant growth mindset. If you scored 1, have a good long think about your career choice!

Do you need to change your mindset?

Are mindsets changeable?

Mindsets aren't themselves fixed. They're beliefs, remember, and beliefs are changeable. One of Barry's daughters realised this when she was 14.

> *Clare had been the unfortunate beneficiary of relentless praise from her adoring parents in her infancy, and it showed in her gradual aversion to challenges, failure, and hard work. In an idle holiday moment on a French campsite she asked her father what he was reading. He told her – a recent research paper on mindset (he's very sad). They discussed mindset for a while, and then she said, 'I've got a fixed mindset, haven't I?' She justified her insight with searing honesty, then smiled: 'But I don't have to stay fixed, do I? It's only a belief!' That moment is marked in the family diary as the day Clare set about reinventing herself and committing to her studies with a scary intensity.*

The rest of this Pocketbook consists of a series of strategies and ideas for ensuring that *your* pupils have the best possible chance of creating or further developing growth mindsets during their time with you. If you teach young children, great – start now. If you work with adolescents, it's not too late. Barry started working on his own fixed mindset in his late 30s. It's a work in progress.

The Nature
of Mindset

**Trial and
Error**

 Targeted Effort

 Feedback Trumps
Praise and Prizes

 Going Seriously
'Meta'

 Mind Your
Language

 Growing a Group
Growth Mindset

Trial and Error

Loving the tough stuff

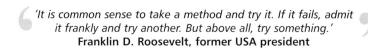

'It is common sense to take a method and try it. If it fails, admit
it frankly and try another. But above all, try something.'
Franklin D. Roosevelt, former USA president

This chapter will explore why many of the things children and adults tend to avoid are actually just the sort of things we should embrace. You'll see how the following inter-connected opportunities and experiences can help grow growth mindsets:

- High-challenge tasks
- Failure
- Errors and mistakes

The power of failure

As a teacher, try to help your pupils to see all true learning as a rumbustious process of trial, error and eventual (and provisional) achievement.

Our failures – and those of our pupils – are *events*, not reflections of who we *are*. And all events invite us to learn. By reflecting on what lies behind our failures we can convert them into powerful learning experiences. Great achievers have done this across the centuries, sometimes at heroic levels.

One school Barry visited made the value of failure very explicit to its pupils. Every classroom had an acrostic poster prominently displayed

First
Attempt
In
Learning

Mindset show and tell

> *'I've missed over 9,000 shots in my career. I've lost almost 300 games. Twenty-six times I've been trusted to take the game-winning shot … and missed. I've failed over and over and over again in my life. And that is why I succeed.'*
> **Michael Jordan, basketball legend, from the Nike advert**

Particularly in primary school, 'show-and-tell' is a time-served activity. Pupils bring things in and then show and tell their peers about them. You can give it a growth mindset twist in two different ways and use the technique across the age range.

1. Instruct your pupils to find out about someone who has achieved things through first failing or making mistakes. Ask them to research this person and to bring in a picture to show and a story to tell.

2. Ask your pupils to go away and think about a time when they themselves made a mistake or failed at something but subsequently learnt from this. Ask them to bring in a picture or an object which represents what happened and to be ready to tell the class about the event.

The value of challenge

You know already that challenge is good. It underpins Ofsted's descriptions of outstanding lessons – and rightly so. Actually we've *always* known that challenge is a desirable constituent of a good learning environment. No-one said it better or more succinctly than two researchers from the 1930s:

> 'Children develop only as the environment demands that they develop.'
> **Sherman & Key, 1932**

Well, maybe Harry, a Year 6 pupil in Croydon, said it even better. When Barry asked his class what 'challenge' actually meant, Harry replied:

It's something tough. Not cheap meat tough. It does your 'ead in tough.

Challenge and achievement

Education Professor John Hattie has synthesised thousands of studies to see which school and classroom practices have most influence on pupils' achievement. His readings of the research literature leave him in no doubt about the value of challenge:

> *The presence of challenging learning intentions has multiple consequences. Pupils can be induced to invest greater effort, and invest more of their total capacity than under low demand conditions. Such intellectual engagement involves a desire to engage and understand the world, have an interest in a wide variety of things, and not be put off by complex and challenging problems.*
>
> **(Visible Learning, p 246)**

Challenge and its neuro-roots

Researchers in fields like neuroscience are beginning to reveal just *why* high-challenge tasks lead to high achievement in all skill and knowledge domains.

We'll return to the neuro thing in the next section when we look at the role of sustained effort. For the moment let us keep in mind that learning anything involves laying insulation (in the form of myelin) around individual neurons in linked neural circuits, thereby increasing electrical signal strength, speed and accuracy (brainpower). The more insulation the better. And we build well-insulated neural circuits most efficiently when we deliberately and repeatedly practise activities that are just beyond our current level of accomplishment, refining and improving things as we go.

We need to encourage something called **deliberate practice**.

Deliberate practice – let your reach exceed your grasp

The foremost researcher in the field of developing expertise, K. Anders Ericsson, identifies the nature and role of deliberate practice in this way:

> *The key attribute of deliberate practice is that individuals seek out new challenges that go beyond their current level of reliable achievement – ideally in a safe and optimal learning context that allows immediate feedback and gradual refinement by repetition.*

Development of Professional Expertise, p425

So it's no good just practising things we've already mastered. Practice will not in itself lead to good learning and achievement – and it might have the unwanted effect of hardwiring faulty learning. We must focus on the tough stuff and let our reach exceed our grasp.

Enter our hero, *Challenge*.

Challenge and mindset

But how does the concept of challenge relate to children's mindset specifically? We've already seen from Rowan's aversion to a high-challenge task and Naz's embrace of it, that challenges are viewed differently by different people:

For those with fixed mindsets, challenges carry with them the prospect of 'failure' and the consequent 'exposure' of a limited intelligence.

For those with a growth mindset, challenges are ideal learning opportunities – a chance to extend their knowledge and skills beyond their current levels.

When children learn that sticking at tough, challenging tasks leads to changes to their brains that make them smarter, we have a way of disrupting fixed mindsets and reinforcing growth mindsets. Exciting new research is beginning to make this process visible, as you will see on the next page.

Neural responses to error

In 2011 Jason Moser and his colleagues at Michigan State University identified a neural mechanism that helps explain just why having a growth mindset helps you cope better with mistakes: a growth mindset is associated with *Pe amplitude* – a brain signal that reflects conscious attention to errors and improved subsequent performance.

When learners with growth mindsets encounter mistakes their electrical brain activity is far greater than those with fixed mindsets:

Growth mindset brains start vigorously *detecting* errors, *processing* errors and *correcting* errors.

Fixed mindset brains seem to start tuning out corrective feedback and closing down neural activity when things get tough – feedback about errors seems too distressing for them to handle.

Tell your pupils about this research. It might help them to grasp how their brain actually *behaves* differently when they simply *believe* different things about it!

Linking challenge to pupils' experiences

Ask your pupils to brainstorm ways in which having a go and sticking at challenging tasks resulted in their achieving something they valued. Expect the following sorts of examples to arise:

Learning to ride a bike or to swim

Getting a high grade in a test and subject they find tricky

Landing a holiday job

Managing to juggle three apples

Winning a school chess tournament

Mastering number tables

Now ask them what's changed 'inside' them, as a result of this dogged practice – ie even when they're not doing the identified achievement.

Use the ensuing discussion to teach them that their neural circuits are now wired differently – and pretty much permanently: even if they don't ride a bike for a decade, they'll pick the skill up again very quickly when they do; the social skills they developed in landing a holiday job will come in useful again.

The power of failure

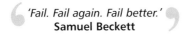

'Fail. Fail again. Fail better.'
Samuel Beckett

Whatever experiences your pupils recall from their own personal stories of achievement, repeated failures will have been a big part of it. In fact, learning only happens through reflection and acting on the experience of failure – otherwise we're simply practising past learning.

The philosopher and cognitive scientist Daniel Dennett makes a similar point in his book, *Intuition Pumps and Other Tools for Thinking*:

> *'[As a species] … we share the benefits our individual brains have won by their individual histories of trial and error.'*

He reveals his own growth mindset in the observation that admitting to errors holds no real horrors:

> *Generous-spirited people appreciate your giving them the opportunity to help. Mean-spirited people enjoy showing you up. Let them! Either way we all win.*

Mistakes are brilliant!

*Mike once heard a famous musician speaking about teaching. **'Mistakes are brilliant!'** he bellowed, radiating energy and enthusiasm. The entire audience were emboldened, raised up and filled with power and potential. They were a group of school leaders; people who are constantly told that mistakes will not be tolerated. The change in the atmosphere was tangible. Mistakes were being recast as the greatest boon to learning and creativity ever imagined.*

You can tap into this same vein of thinking, inspiring your pupils to think big. Tell them that mistakes are brilliant. Make them believe it. You'll change their mindsets.

Wimbledon High School famously instituted a 'Failure Week' as one way of teaching their pupils about the power of failure. It has proved to be a hugely powerful experience for those involved, though not without controversy – we're suspicious of failure in our society!

Modelling mistakes

You're a teacher. As you already know, teaching involves making plenty of mistakes. This is the fastest route to getting better at the job. You try something. It doesn't work. You think about why it didn't work and then you try something else instead. That works and so you keep using it, making refinements as you go.

The result is that most teachers have extensive experience of growth mindsets in relation to their job. And even if you've ended up stuck in a fixed mindset you can easily change things by challenging yourself to do something different next lesson.

The beauty of this is that you can share your experiences with the pupils you teach. You can talk to them about mistakes you have made during the course of your career, and how this has helped you to get better. If you're feeling brave you can even talk about mistakes made during the current lesson. This can lead to a whole-class growth mindset in which you and your pupils work together as one, sharing the learning load.

A quick experience of failure and success

You can get your pupils working towards a growth mindset by setting up activities deliberately involving trial and error. In maths and science this happens all the time. In fact, the entire history of progress in these subjects is a history of growth mindsets. Many scientists used to believe that a mysterious element called 'phlogiston' caused things to burn. It was only the committed growth mindsets of subsequent researchers which allowed us to discover the truth (for now) – that oxygen is the culprit!

Here are five trial and error activities you can use:

* Set pupils a problem and give them free rein to try out different solutions
* Pupils work in groups on a problem. One pupil records the trials and errors which come about
* Give all your pupils a rough book to practise work in first
* Encourage pupils to include trial and error in their written work. For instance, by starting again, showing working out and writing notes in the margin
* Model trial and error in front of the whole class, talking them through as you go, eg: *'So, this mistake has been helpful to me because I learned from it that…'*

Logging mistakes

The simple technique of writing mistakes down in a log can help pupils to develop a growth mindset.

Logging has two big benefits. First, it normalises the process of making mistakes, pulling it back out from under the accumulated bushels of the fixed mindset. Second, it gives pupils an opportunity to reflect on what they learnt from their mistakes. You might provide a pro-forma a bit like this:

What was the mistake?	Why was it useful?	What did you learn from it?
I got question 7 wrong, even though I can do this sort of problem in my sleep.	It was only a practice test, so I can do better in the actual exam.	To check that the Q is actually asking what I assume it's asking.

Of course, the more challenging you make your activities, the more likely that pupils will make mistakes. And the more likely they will learn as a result.

Stories of success

Don't limit thinking about challenge and the benefits of making mistakes to the classroom. Growth mindset success stories abound. Tell your students how David Beckham and Jonny Wilkinson used to practise for hours every day to make the most of their talent. Tell them how Robert M. Pirsig's novel *Zen and the Art of Motorcycle Maintenance* was rejected by 121 publishers. It has sold five million copies worldwide.

Set homework that gets pupils focusing on growth mindsets outside of school:

- Research a famous achiever and find out how long it took that person to develop their ideas or skills and how many mistakes they made in the process. Aim for the 'natural-born geniuses', eg Beethoven, Newton, Kelly Holmes, Sylvia Plath

- Study the backgrounds of late developers who finally made it: novelist JK Rowling, footballer Ricki Lambert, musician Sixto Rodriguez, Winston Churchill, etc

- Try something new for a fortnight (eg kicking with their non-dominant foot, tackling a really tough piece of sight-reading, exploring a genre they normally avoid) and record their mistakes, experiences and learning during that period

The artist's approach

Have you ever made a sketch? Usually artists start working in pencil. It's easy to make changes with pencil – you just rub a bit out and then start again. Every time artists do that they are getting closer to what is in their mind. They are using the mistakes to get better, challenging themselves to create something out of nothing.

The idea of making improvements in real-time is a powerful one. Here are three ways to introduce it to your lessons:

1. During activities, call for 'review time' during which pupils look at what they have done and work out what they can alter.
2. Start calling all classwork 'work-in-development'.
3. Use activities in which an element repeats, allowing pupils to get better as they go, eg in a German lesson you could invite students to explain their opinion to three people in a row. Each time they will be able to refine and improve their speech.

All the above involves *effort*, the subject of the next section.

Targeted Effort

Effort is important but problematic

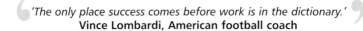
'The only place success comes before work is in the dictionary.'
Vince Lombardi, American football coach

People with growth mindsets know that effort is where it's at. This insight can be reverse-engineered too: people who come to see the value of effort are well on the way to developing growth mindsets. So it makes sense for teachers to encourage effortful learning in their pupils. However there are at least three overlapping problems with the concept of effort:

1. It's not well understood.
2. It's not easy to operationalise – ie to make it visible and measurable.
3. It's not terribly sexy.

This chapter attempts to remedy all three, and suggest ways in which you might adapt and apply these remedies in your classroom.

Understanding effort – work vs learning

> *'All great artists and thinkers are great workers, indefatigable not only in inventing, but also in rejecting, sifting, transforming, ordering.'*
> **Friedrich Nietzsche, melancholic philosopher**

Since they first attended pre-school, your pupils will have heard adults exhorting them to 'work harder'. But what do they think this means and what does it look like? It's important that they don't see this advice as an appeal to 'empty effort' – spending hours doing something unpleasant and with little good learning to show for it. If they understand 'harder' as meaning only 'longer', they lose the essential quality of 'work' being mental or physical effort *directed towards the achievement of something*.

It might be helpful to reduce your use of the word 'work' and ramp up your use of the word 'learning' – something which more clearly brings personal benefits to the pupil:

'Get on with your ~~work~~ *learning* Year 3' or 'You've been ~~working~~ *learning* really hard today Year 9'.

Understanding effort – what does 'working hard' mean?

Consider devoting a lesson to an enquiry around the concept of 'work' or 'effort'. If you're familiar with the Philosophy for Children approach, you could facilitate an enquiry on the theme. Choose an age-appropriate work-related stimulus, eg:

- The story of the Labours of Sisyphus
- Aesop's fable, The Tortoise and the Hare
- A picture-book with hard work as a central plotline
- The sinister 'Arbeit Macht Frei' entrance to Auschwitz

Alternatively, simply ask directly: *'What do you think 'working hard' really means?'* or *'Is it important to work hard? Why?'* Probe and prompt for examples, counter-examples, reasons, evidence, assumptions, implications, consequences, etc. Aim to:

1. Challenge or deepen platitudes (eg *'Because work is good.'* *'Really? What about working hard to become a successful murderer?'*).
2. Expose naïve theories (eg *'Work means doing something unpleasant.'* *'Always? What about working to do better at something you enjoy?'*).
3. Help pupils construct their own improved understandings.

If you don't sweat it ...

> *Barry spent his schooldays avoiding all 'work' on the grounds that exams and other indicators of academic success should be (in his damaged mind) a measure of pure intellectual ability. So working for them was tantamount to cheating! He was the victim of having been described as 'very bright' as a young child, and the effortless success of his big-fish primary school years gave way to the academic disaster-zone of his secondary school years. Even then he carefully preserved the illusion of brightness, ostentatiously professing his disdain for work and his passion for chess – a game associated with 'true intelligence'!*

In pursuit of a classful of growth mindsets, your task is to help your pupils connect effort and achievement via the mediating concept we explored earlier – challenge. In other words:

If I don't sweat it, I won't get it!

Neural learning

To understand better the links between challenge, effort and achievement and their role in creating growth mindsets, let's get back to neural basics. Here's the humble neuron:

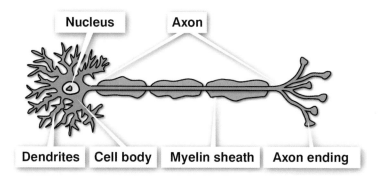

Firing on all cylinders

Every one of our thoughts, emotions and actions involves sending electrical signals down a chain of neurons – a bit like passing the flame in an Olympic torch relay. So learning happens when neurons get it together in a wild revelry of over-heated nerve fibres:

- Some internal or external event (eg a thought or an experience) triggers two neurons to fire together

- Further stimulation leads to a third neuron firing and a linked circuit is formed

- In future, given the appropriate stimulus, if one neuron fires all three fire together. As the saying goes, *'Neurons that fire together, wire together'*

- The web of interconnectivity spreads through the brain as more connections are made

- The more often the linked circuit fires (ie the refined skill is practised), the more insulating myelin gets laid down – increasing the speed, accuracy and automaticity of the learned skill. The greater the practice the fewer the short circuits, outages and other breakdowns in learner power

- When the learner experiences improvement, it's reinforced by a pleasurable release of dopamine, increasing attention and motivation to attempt the task again

The sum of the parts

In their effortful struggle to master a complex skill or domain of knowledge, get your pupils to understand what's going on inside them:

1. Picture it	Get a sense of the whole (*what does the future full accomplishment look like?*).
2. Chunk it down	Break down the whole into its several parts (*what are its constituent circuits?*).
3. Easy does it	Address each part individually (*can I master each circuit?*).
4. Chunk it up	Rebuild the parts (*can I slowly put the mastered circuits together into increasingly large connected circuits?*).
5. Check it	Assess for accuracy (*is it correct? Any modifications needed?*).
6. Hardwire it	Practise, practise, practise (*can I repeat the process enough times, making increasingly refined adjustments to ensure I'm fixing the right circuit?*).

You will see exactly this process at work, probably intuitively, in an experienced music teacher, mathematician, potter, athlete, poet … ie in every domain of achievement.

Making effort visible

Even when your pupils have a reasonable understanding of what effort is, at an abstract or a neural level, do they know what it looks like in their own lives? One way to **make effort visible** is to give pupils a set of effort-related criteria to use to assess their recent work. Here are seven criteria shaped as questions:

1. *Have you thought hard about how to respond to challenges?*
2. *Have you kept going when the work became difficult?*
3. *Have you tried to take the easiest route? Is 'easiest' best on this occasion?*
4. *Is the work the best you could have produced? Why?*
5. *Does the work suggest someone thinking hard and challenging themselves?*
6. *What do you notice happens to you when the task becomes hard?*
7. *What do you do when you find yourself becoming frustrated? Why do you think you react that way? Is it helpful? How?*

These questions encourage pupils to think about effort in a precise and meaningful way. In the process, their understanding of the concept will develop.

Don't let effort grades be blunt tools

Many schools use effort grades as a way of rewarding pupils' sustained commitment and work ethic, or as a 'wake-up call'. Effort grades can be very helpful in creating growth mindsets since they locate achievement in the reality of hard work, not the mystery of 'ability'. However, their power evaporates entirely when:

Effort descriptions are contaminated with fixed mindset terminology, as in 'Standard of work doesn't reflect *ability*'. If you're talking only about effort, why invoke alternative explanations for performance?	Unsophisticated effort descriptions are used, eg simple 5-point scales which don't help pupils to see what each level's grade actually *means*.	There's an assumption that teachers know better than the pupils how hard the pupils have worked, eg '*Latifa has worked hard this term.*'
Instead: Keep focused on the effort!	**Instead:** Don't just label – assist! (See idea on following page.)	**Instead:** In combination with the previous point, trust pupils to provide their own effort grades. Let them do the work!

Meaningful effort grades

So how can you tap into the power of effort grades?

One secondary school English teacher in the midlands resolved to improve her department's use of effort grades by making them more meaningful to pupils. Each of five effort grades (A-E) was broken down into six descriptions – ie 30 descriptions in total – reflecting such effort-sensitive strands as argumentation, care in writing, depth of thought, participation, observation of deadlines, and initiative. Here's how the 'care in writing' strand was evidenced:

A – revealed considerable scrutiny of writing; carefully proof-read for errors
B – revealed sufficient care in writing to prevent or correct many errors
C – revealed some attention to writing to prevent or correct some errors
D – prevention and correction of errors left mostly to the teacher
E – little attempt to prevent and correct errors

With some thought you can easily construct an effort grade schedule that meets the needs of your pupils' age or your subject area. Teachers that do so report outstanding results in terms of their pupils' motivation, work-rate – and honesty!

Differentiating effort grades

As in the previous example, you can provide pupils with a breakdown of the total task and get them to give their own effort grades. Or you can get them to 'effort-differentiate' the whole task themselves. This way they learn that in any task we can put effort in by doing different things.

For example, when learning to play the piano we could spend time working on exercises, reading music or practising extended pieces. Help your pupils think about the different ways they need to put in effort by breaking a task down and awarding effort grades for each segment. You could divide writing a history essay like this:

- Researching the subject
- Planning the essay
- Writing the essay
- Editing and redrafting the essay
- Acting on feedback

Giving an effort grade for each segment will help pupils think about effort more effectively. They will start to see the different things effort encompasses.

Making effort sexy

Often, students see effort as a slog – something they have to get through and which is best avoided wherever possible. A way to counter this perception and to make effort more appealing is by giving your pupils a clearer sense of how effort, hard work and persistence lead to rewards and benefits in the long-run.

Internal changes: Remind them of the brain-events and changes that occur when they engage in effortful activity (see pages 49 and 50).

External changes: Ask pupils to pick something they've learnt either in school or outside and to list everything they've done which has contributed to their learning. Next, ask them to insert these items into a shape like the one on the next page, with the basics along the bottom, followed by the next level, building to the next and so on.

Making effort sexy

In this example, a pupil has picked learning to play football well enough to get into a local team.

Where I am at now ▶ Good enough to play for Borough United U-14s

Learned how to shoot under preasure

Learned how to defend corners

Learned how to keep fit

Learned how to run fast with the ball

Learned how to hit a good cross

Beginning ▶ Learned what football is

Learned how to kick a ball

Learned to be part of a team

Learned how to pass

This is a great way to visualise the benefits of effort over the long-run. Now what block/s can be added at the top?

Giving effort status

If you want lots of effort from your pupils, you need to give it real status in your classroom:

'Well done for trying different approaches when you were stuck.'

'I like the fact that you saw the difficulties as an interesting challenge.'

'The way you tried harder when things became more difficult was excellent.'

'Well done for keeping going and not giving up – that's what we want to see!'

'Excellent persistence on this piece of work – as shown by the crossings out.'

In each example above you are reinforcing the effort instead of the end product. This helps pupils to see that effort is valued in your classroom – not just getting something finished or making it look nice.

Tapping into 'divine dissatisfaction'

From great effort, great wonders spring. This is one interpretation of what dancer and choreographer Martha Graham meant by *'divine dissatisfaction'*. There is something masochistically enjoyable about not being *quite* content with one's present performance. It holds open the heavenly prospect of being even better tomorrow!

A simple way to help pupils appreciate this idea is to have a brief reflection at the end of every lesson in which they discuss what *dissatisfied* them about their intellectual, creative or productive work. Begin by revisiting the dissatisfactions of the previous lesson and asking them to think about how they have targeted their effort in response to this.

If you get any answers along the lines of *'Nothing dissatisfied me'*, don't take them as a cop-out. Instead, say: *'OK, I'll make the next lesson a lot more challenging then; thanks for letting me know!'* Divine dissatisfaction will soon develop!

Asking students what dissatisfied them requires *them* to give *you* quality **feedback** – the subject of our next chapter.

Feedback Trumps
Praise and Prizes

Abandoning cherished practices

Bear with us! In this chapter we could be nibbling away at some of your most cherished practices. In some cases this might be less of a nibble than a savage chomp. We will be questioning from first principles the role of praise, stickers, reward schedules, prizes, 'self-esteem' and other off-shoots of behaviourism and 1970s Californian culture. This isn't because stickers, praise etc don't work or aren't sometimes recommended by people who should know better. They often *do* achieve certain things. But they do so at a cost. The cost is to a learner's intrinsic motivation and growth mindset.

We will suggest alternative routes to growth mindset ends. We're aiming for intrinsically-motivated learners, not extrinsically-motivated sticker-junkies.

As we write, we will look back guiltily on our own past practices. Barry remembers how he used to buy industrial quantities of fun-sized Mars Bars as rewards for his pupils. He's since improved his practice. Please do as he now says, not as he once did…

The nature of feedback

Feedback is *information provided about any aspect of someone's behaviour, performance or understanding*. It can be provided by anyone (eg a teacher) or anything (eg the score you get in an online quiz). You can also generate your own feedback – eg when reflecting on a lesson's success and the possible reasons for it.

The link between feedback and our previous growth mindset heroes, *challenge* and *effort*, is this: challenging, effortful tasks need rapid, high quality feedback in order to:

- Keep learners engaged
- Help learners spot weaknesses in their performances (there's no point practising and embedding flawed skills or understandings)
- Help learners know when they're getting something right

When **challenge**, **effort** and **feedback** operate in harmony, learners begin to see their skills and understanding develop in real time – literally growing their abilities and exposing as an absurdity the notion that these are fixed.

The importance of feedback

As a teacher, you're giving and receiving feedback throughout the day. Because it's omnipresent, it's not surprising that feedback plays a major role in creating, maintaining and changing mindsets. We know from the research on formative assessment that:

 the best feedback you can give your pupils will be the feedback that provides them with the most helpful information.

How can you be sure you're giving the sort of information that feeds a growth mindset and starves a fixed mindset?

Growth vs fixed mindset feedback

When feedback is oriented explicitly towards guiding future behaviour, growth mindsets flourish. But to do this you will need to win three linked battles, with forces ranged as follows:

Information (eg 'You need to ...')	vs	Judgment 'That's a weak answer'
Future (eg 'The next time, try ...')	vs	Past 'You failed that'
Behaviour (eg 'Did you really challenge yourself here?')	vs	Ability 'You're an A-grade pupil – I'd hoped for more from you')

Always go for the first of each of these. That way you'll be providing **Information** to guide **Future Behaviour** – not judging children on the basis of fixed abilities. To see the impact of this, try the exercise on the next page.

Evaluating feedback

If you rate the following three pieces of feedback according to the **growth mindset feedback criteria** we've just introduced, you'll probably end up with these outcomes:

Feedback offered	Informational?	Future-oriented?	Behavioural?
A. That's brilliant Marcus	✔ (sort of)	✘	✔ (sort of)
B. OK Nat, but what if you …?	✔	✔	✔
C. Jaidev you're a superstar!	✘	✘	✘

And now rated according to the **fixed mindset feedback criteria**:

Feedback offered	Judgment?	Past?	Ability?
A. That's brilliant Marcus	✔	✔	✘
B.OK Nat, but what if you …?	✘	✘	✘
C. Jaidev you're a superstar!	✔	✔ (job's done!)	✔

Try evaluating some feedback of your own using these criteria. (See the bad praise challenge on page 67 for a way of making this fun and slightly adversarial!)

The problem with praise

Arguably, praise of the 'You're a superstar / genius / smart cookie' sort is barely feedback at all. It gives students no information about the task, or how they tackled it, or how they might take ownership of its mastery. Instead, this kind of 'fixed' praise risks closing down future learning by:

* Inviting complacency (*'Geniuses always excel, don't they?'*)
* Locating the purpose of learning as pleasing someone else (*'Should I be doing this for my teacher, or myself?'*)
* Creating resentment (*'I dislike people who don't say I'm a genius.'*)
* Inspiring a fear of future failure (*'Can I ever evoke that level of praise again?'*)

It's all too easy in the hurly burly of classroom life to praise a pupil for something they didn't actually find difficult; we've known for some time* that this can serve to *lower* personal expectations of performance.

> 'He was pleased with that?! (Maybe it's because I'm not capable of doing any better.')

*Eg Morine-Dershimer's research in the '80s

But kids love praise!

> 'If we are not accountable [to ourselves], we shall wander the world seeking someone to explain ourselves to, someone to absolve us and tell us we have done well.'
>
> **Nietzsche**

Yes, pupils love praise. Don't we all? We might also enjoy sweets, cigarettes and huge, calorie-laden breakfasts, but it doesn't mean they're good for us. Praise, prizes and performance grades all act as **extrinsic reinforcers**, focusing on the outcomes of learning rather than the **intrinsic satisfactions** of the task itself.

As we said earlier, it's not that extrinsic reinforcers don't work, they often do. But they work at the expense of something much more precious than behavioural compliance – your learners' intrinsic motivation and desire to grow their skills, knowledge and competencies. We know this from decades of research – rewards have hidden costs. So your sticker charts and reward schedules will probably get short-term results, but they won't turn your pupils on to learning – they are more likely to turn them into sticker-seekers, or individuals who'll go through life seeking meaning in others' affirmation, absolution or judgment.

Bad praise monitors

There is value in being explicit with your pupils about why you're not (any longer) going to be giving them the wrong sort of praise. Better still, get them to train you:

Bad Praise Challenge
Invite your pupils to spot times you seem to give fixed mindset praise and to issue you with a 'bad praise challenge'. Use the second table on page 64 to test out their hunches.

- If they get a full score – 3 out of 3, you could put 20p into a Comic Relief tin or let your lapse count towards an intrinsic motivator, eg a lesson with content of their choosing

- If they register a false challenge, scoring 0 or 1 out of 3, they must perform a growth mindset sanction of your choice

- 2 out of 3 is a draw – a warning shot but no sanction in either direction

They'll love trying to keep you honest in your avoidance of fixed mindset praise and arguing the toss over the score will result in high-level conversation about learning.

Reframing praise

In pursuit of growth mindsets it's possibly best to avoid the word 'praise' with all its fuzziness and unhelpful associations. Instead, you're more likely to provide information to guide future behaviour when you offer positive (and critical) **feedback**, or **recognition**, or **encouragement**. Or simply show intense *interest* in your pupils' learning. To see this in action, have a look at this description of the high-achieving Fiennes children remembering their parents' habitual response to their children's work:

> *'There was always analysis, be it homework or a picture. Anything that was created, there was immediately a discussion about it. Could it be this? Or should we try this or that? Never, 'That's lovely darling, let's put it on the shelf.'*
> **Fiennes family, The Guardian, 3 December 2011**

Children aren't traumatised by adults who show critical interest in their learning, and who avoid mindless affirmations. But for those who've been raised on a diet of hyperbolic praise this lesson might be hard won. Stick with it.

It's time for retraining

For many of us, promoting growth mindsets means making some adjustments ourselves first. Mike found that in his teaching he had to alter some of the ways in which he gave feedback by avoiding general praise and instead focusing on effort and developmental comments.

One way to retrain yourself to give better feedback is to learn some feedback sentence starters. Here are a few you can begin using right away:

✔ 'Let me tell you why I think you have persevered with this piece of work…'

✔ 'This is an interesting choice you have made here…'

✔ 'It's clear from the number of changes the work has been through that you have…'

✔ 'This work suggests that you might now start thinking about…'

✔ 'I can identify the effort you have put into this from…'

Focused feedback

Feedback is most effective when it focuses on something specific. This gives pupils the opportunity to make a useful change and provides them with the information needed to do this. Really good growth mindset feedback focuses on things such as:

(1) The relative levels of effort put into different aspects of the work.

'You have put a high level of effort into the start of your work but this has then dropped. Next time, try to keep your effort levels high from start to finish.'

(2) Suggestions about what to do next and why it might improve the work.

'Have you considered including more examples in your work? These will improve your writing by making your points clearer.'

(3) Questions which cause pupils to reflect on what they have done and how they have done it.

'What made you choose to approach the work in this way?'

(4) Identification of the thought processes employed and what these led to.

'I can see from your working out that you have been practising applying the formulae we learnt. This is good; keep it up.'

(5) Challenges to do things differently or to do things which are more difficult.

'How could you have made the task more challenging for yourself?'

Turning pupils into feedback givers (1)

If you can get your pupils *giving* effective feedback then you will have helped transform their thinking. No longer will they be moving along trapped in a fixed mindset. Instead they will be actively aware of the intimate connection between quality feedback and quality learning.

A good way to achieve this is through **peer-assessment**. Create a grid like the one below and ask pupils to use it to assess their partner's work:

Explain the evidence you can find that your partner has put effort into her work.	
How can your partner improve her thinking?	Eg: Alice could use a rough book to sketch out some different ideas before she starts. Then she could make some mistakes and learn from these at the beginning.
What can your partner do to improve her work?	

Turning pupils into feedback givers (2)

Another way to help students internalise the criteria which underpin effective feedback is through **self-assessment**. Give pupils a checklist like the one below, which they use to assess what they have done and on which they can indicate evidence of having successfully met each of the criteria.

Criteria	Where's the Evidence?
The work was challenging and pushed my thinking	
I thought about what I was doing and tried out different approaches	Eg: At the beginning I thought about three different ways to start in my head and then chose the one I liked best.
I kept going when things were difficult	
The work shows me putting a lot of effort into what I was doing	Eg: I have written more than last time and the last three paragraphs all contain more information than normal for me.
I can identify when I pushed myself and when I didn't	

Real-time continuous feedback

We know that feedback is the gold dust that makes learning happen. It is one of the most important ways to ensure pupil progress. You can accelerate the pace of progress by giving feedback in real-time.

During a groupwork task ask pupils from each group to bring you a 'status update' every five minutes or so. On hearing where each group is at you can give feedback which will help them to improve. At the next 'status update' you can ask for an explanation of how your last piece of feedback was used before giving the next piece.

Repeating the process three or four times during a task will help all groups to make swift and significant progress.

Interview feedback

It isn't always easy to speak with every pupil individually. However, if you can make time for it the results can be impressive. Try this:

Create a grid like the one on the next page containing different keywords and statements which are indicative of excellent feedback and which connect to the idea of growth mindsets. Next, invite pupils in your class to join you for a learning interview.

During the interview, talk to the pupils about their work, their thinking and their learning. As they respond, encourage them to use the grid to help them formulate their answers. Through this process, pupils will do two things:

1. Analyse and reflect on their own performance.
2. Practise giving high-quality feedback which will eventually lead to their internalising the associated language.

Interview feedback example

All the words or statements in the grid below connect to growth mindsets.
Pupils can use them as prompts when talking to you. Or, they can develop their own
responses based on some of the ideas contained in the grid.

I can identify a mistake I made and how I used it to learn	Using failure to my advantage	Perseverance
Keeping Going	I have put the most effort possible into my work	Trying different ways to solve things
Seeking out challenge	Determination	I can give examples of how my learning connects to the effort I have put in and the way I have kept going

Auto-feedback

A well-known technique for changing how we think is called positive visualisation. This is where we imagine a future situation going really well. We see ourselves dealing with it and succeeding in it. In a sense, we're giving ourselves feedback on our futures! You can adapt this technique to help students develop a growth mindset.

Ask your pupils to imagine themselves taking on a complete growth mindset from the next morning onwards and to write a story, *'Me From Tomorrow…'*, exploring what that would be like. How would they feel, act, think, behave and learn?

I woke up at seven and rolled over in bed. My alarm clock was telling me it was time to get up for school. I pushed myself out of bed and opened the curtains. It was a beautiful morning and I said to myself: 'Today will be different. Today I am going to learn from every mistake I make.'

The next thing I knew I was downstairs eating my breakfast. The milk was too cold in my cereal. So, I thought, tomorrow why don't I take the milk out of the fridge before I have my shower? That way it will be at just the right temperature…'

To support pupils who find the activity difficult, suggest specific situations to write about, eg certain lessons they find difficult, playing a sport, working with others, etc.

Tracking feedback

Given everything we have said about feedback, one thing we have missed out is the fact that it can be hard to track. Verbal feedback slips off into the ether; written feedback can be lost in the pages of an exercise book.

Not to worry! Help is at hand in the form of a target tracker sheet. Simply print out a sheet of A4 with the following columns:

Date	Feedback	Your Thoughts
3rd Nov	I should think carefully about new ideas and how to connect them to old ones.	I agree. I am making an effort to embrace new ideas and see where they go.

Pupils can stick this to the inside cover of their exercise books and fill it in as time goes by. This way both you and they can keep a track of what feedback has been given and whether it has had a positive effect. If you're being explicit about mindset with them, ask them to reflect on the effect of the feedback on their mindset.

Making the grade?

Finally, a few words about the relationship between growth mindset feedback and 'target grades'. It's a troubled relationship. The secondary sector especially is awash with practices and advice that link baseline data with actual grades, target grades, predicted grades, and the like. We'll leave you to reflect on these cautionary, insightful and aspirational words from the blog of John Tomsett, headteacher of Huntington School, York.

Posted by
**John
Tomsett**

Once you start to think hard about what Dweck says you begin to question everything about what you do as a school leader. If Dweck is right – and in my personal experience I think she is – then setting students grades as targets is deeply flawed. The subject leaders of our two most successful A levels, the ones which are about to explode out the top of the ALPs** thermometer and make an awful mess, both fessed up to me this autumn that they don't look at students' targets, they don't consciously differentiate, they just teach to A* standard all of the time to all of the students. Go figure... **johntomsett.wordpress.com**

**National database looking at annual 'A' level performance

Going Seriously
'Meta'

It's the learner's job to learn

In the extract alongside, Guardian columnist Tim Dowling describes the parental dilemma of knowing that the job of learning lies with the learner, but not knowing how to get the learner to know this!

As with A-levels, so with mindset; and so too with learning at any age, from the very first days of school to the final ones.

> The Guardian, 25th May 2013
>
> ... His A-level revision, we explain, must be a matter for him alone; only he can summon up the required commitment, we cannot want it for him. We tell him this between 30 and 40 times a day, shaking him awake to deliver the message if necessary.

A focus on challenge, trial and error, effort and feedback will all be valuable as routes towards a classful of growth mindsets, but *most* valuable when your pupils come to value these things for themselves. This happens when they start **thinking about their own thinking**, and **learning about their own learning** – ie when they go seriously, bravely, gloriously 'meta'. Read on ....

The nature of meta-learning

The prefix 'meta' has Greek roots and means going above or beyond something. So **meta-learning** is being aware of how you are learning and **meta-thinking** is reflecting actively on the kind of thinking you are doing. This means selecting tools and strategies that can help improve your expanding mind.

It's not difficult to see why 'going meta' leads to more effective learning, and why meta-cognitive processes underpin most of the really powerful influences on academic achievement. Especially when tasks are demanding, the quality of pupils' meta-cognitive skills rather than their intellectual abilities becomes the chief determinant of their learning outcomes*. Learnable skills trump fixed abilities at every turn.

In this chapter we will explore ways of acquiring the meta-cognitive tools and strategies to go in pursuit of growth mindsets.

*John Hattie, Visible Learning

Motivation and volition

Having the will to go meta is not enough. Returning to Dowling Junior, he might in reality be strongly *motivated* to get good A-levels, but simply lacking the wherewithal to put this motivation into practice:

Motivation
Really wanting something – having the will to achieve it.

Volition
Really committing to something by putting the 'wanting' into action – having the willpower to achieve it.

To grow as a learner we need both **motivation** and **volition**. One without the other is useless.

The next two pages outline a new and research-tested approach to reconciling motivation and volition called **mental contrasting**. This is a meta-cognitive tool invented by psychology professor Gabriele Oettingen (http://psych.nyu.edu/oettingen) and applied by Angela Duckworth in schools and other settings.

MOTIVATION   VOLITION

Mental contrasting

In her research Oettingen found that people tend to use three strategies when setting goals. Only the third one works:

Strategy	Description	Example of tools
1. Indulging (beloved of optimists)	Imagining an ideal future and everything that goes with it – eg getting four As at A-level, relieved teachers, smug parents, the glittering prize of a place at Oxbridge	Aspirational posters (*'Dare to believe!'*, *'To think it is to achieve it'*, *'Because you're worth it'*)
2. Dwelling (characteristic of pessimists)	Imagining all the obstacles en route to achieving your goals – eg your feckless teachers, the vagaries of the OCR Philosophy A-level exam, etc	Listing the obstacles and all those bright former pupils who missed their grades and are now working in call-centres
3. Mental contrasting (used by achievers)	Integrating the first two strategies, so that future and reality lead to do-able 'implementation intentions'	*'If… then…'* statements and rule-setting (see next page)

Mental contrasting in action

To get the best out of indulging and dwelling, get your pupils to connect the obstacles to their goals with possible solutions. **If… then** statements are very useful here:

- *'If I'm tempted to go out with my mates midweek, **then** I will decide for the next three months only to go out on Saturday nights.'* (Reuben, Y13)

- *'If I can't attend extra tuition sessions, **then** I will make greater use of course textbooks and YouTube videos.'* (Chloe, Y11)

- *'If I'm struggling to keep up in this maths set, **then** I will go through each lesson with Dad at home.'* (Eloise, Y6)

- *'If my best friend won't play with me anymore, **then** I will start to make new friends.'* (Yasmin, Y1)

Mental contrasting works by reducing the time pupils spend fantasising and instead increasing their thinking about practical ways of getting round the obstacles. Making up 'rules' that will work for them is a way of fronting up to their more primitive drives and appetites. Rules are a meta-cognitive substitute for willpower, providing courses of predetermined action to follow when temptation calls.

Making metacognition the objective

Whenever we want our pupils to learn something or to cultivate a certain habit, we have to begin by increasing their awareness of the thing in question.

One way to get pupils thinking about their thinking is to have two learning objectives every lesson. Some teachers call this 'split-screen learning'. The first learning will concern the content and skills you want pupils to learn and use. The second objective will be about some aspect of meta-cognition, eg:

- **LO 1**: To investigate what life was like in Roman London
- **LO 2**: To think about how we make decisions when we are investigating a new topic

Doing this over a long period of time should result in meta-cognition becoming second nature to your pupils.

Meta-feedback

We've already seen the power of feedback in supporting the development of growth mindsets. You can enhance this by incorporating a meta-element in your feedback prompts. Try these, adapting the language to suit the age of your pupils:

Task level

- *Does this answer meet the success criteria?*
- *Could you elaborate on (or say a bit more about) this answer?*
- *What's the tricky part in this task?*

Process level

- *What strategies are you using?*
- *What other questions could you ask about this task?*
- *Have you done anything similar to this before?*

Self-regulation level

- *What would be the best way of checking your work?*
- *How could you reflect on these answers?*
- *What aspect of this work could you now teach to others?*

Know your own mind

Thinking about thinking means being consciously aware of our own minds and what we are doing with them. This is difficult for students to achieve and can require extended periods of intensive effort.

A way to assist them in this process is to provide something which can act as a scaffold. Similar to meta-feedback prompts, a set of comprehension self-check questions is a useful example:

- *Do you understand what the writer is trying to do?*
- *How is the writing affecting your thinking?*
- *What is the meaning of the writing?*
- *What does the writing connect to that you already know?*

Students ask themselves these questions during the course of reading a text. They keep doing so until it becomes second nature.

Taking control of your memory

Memory is at the heart of all knowledge and understanding and can support meta-learning processes. By teaching students memory strategies you can help them to use their minds more effectively – not least by freeing up short-term memory for other things.

Some of the most powerful memory strategies involve making visual images of important content – either physically or by imagining images 'in the mind's eye' (as ever, this improves with practice).

Teach your students the following five memory strategies. Each one will help them take control of their own learning and become more meta-cognitively aware:

1. Mnemonics

2. List-writing

3. Using scrap paper as a 'holding area' for thoughts and information

4. Turning information into stories so it is easier to recall

5. Creating associations between words, images, sounds and smells

Attention! Traffic lights

The traffic lights technique is a variation of a technique used to collect feedback from an entire class at the same time. Provide each student with three pieces of card, roughly the size of a wallet, one red, one orange and one green.

Explain to pupils that they should think about what they understand and what they do not understand during the course of the lesson. They should then put whichever card represents their current status on top of the pile:

- Red card on top = I do not understand
- Orange card on top = I understand some things but not all
- Green card on top = I understand completely

Traffic lights not only allow you to see where all your students are at, they help pupils to internalise the notion of thinking about thinking.

Together we are better

We all have strategies to help us learn more effectively. For example, Mike likes to know the meaning behind things, so when he encounters new ideas he analyses the philosophical structures on which they rest. This helps him to understand more quickly than he would otherwise. Other people like talking aloud to themselves. Verbally re-explaining new ideas helps them to synthesise and assimilate new material.

Expose your students to **different learning strategies** by getting them to discuss the different ways in which they tackle learning. Share your own methods as well.

Maura divided her class into pairs and put three questions on the board:

- What things do you do to make learning easier?
- How do you deal with new ideas and information?
- What strategies do you have that help you with your learning?

She asked students to interview each other in turn, discuss their answers then share their findings with the whole class. Each pair then went on to create a poster for a wall display advertising their tools, techniques and strategies.

Mirror, mirror on the wall

Spending time reflecting on what we have done and why we have done it is an important part of meta-cognition.

Consistent reflection makes it more likely that you will start to think about how you are using your mind and how you could use it differently.

Here are five ways you can build reflection into your lessons:

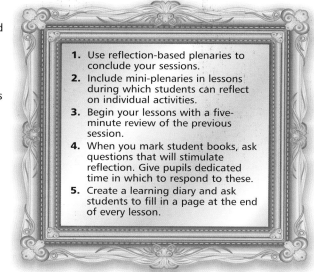

1. Use reflection-based plenaries to conclude your sessions.
2. Include mini-plenaries in lessons during which students can reflect on individual activities.
3. Begin your lessons with a five-minute review of the previous session.
4. When you mark student books, ask questions that will stimulate reflection. Give pupils dedicated time in which to respond to these.
5. Create a learning diary and ask students to fill in a page at the end of every lesson.

Concept mapping

When we cluster things in terms of their similarities, we have a concept of them. 'Courage', 'beauty' and 'change' are all examples of obviously abstract concepts, but 'chair' has the concept of 'chairness' about it too. Concepts underpin our thought. They are the foundations on which our thinking rests.

A key part of learning involves developing an increasingly sophisticated understanding of new and familiar concepts. Different disciplines even have their own subject-specific concepts. For example, 'force' means different things in physics and politics.

Concept maps are a way to help students think meta-cognitively. Simply select a concept relevant to the lesson and ask your pupils to draw a map showing how that concept links to other concepts, people, events, information and so on. This process helps students to visualise the connections inherent in their minds and to critically reflect on these.

A 'Revolution Concept Map'

Here is an example of a simple concept map based on the word 'revolution':

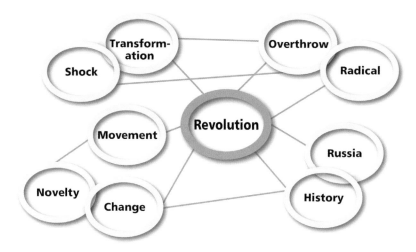

'What if …?' questions

Some years ago Barry recommended the Edward de Bono *'What if …?'* exercise to a conference of primary school teachers (*'What if … all door handles were made of chocolate? … all cars had to be painted yellow?'* etc). The exercise encourages critical and lateral thinking and is usually much enjoyed by children.

A few days later he received some feedback from a Year 4 teacher who'd gone seriously 'meta'. Having done the activity she then asked the class why we might want to ask *'What if …?'* She was delighted with their responses:

- *'It makes us think about something we've never thought about before'*
- *'It gives us new ways of looking at things'*
- *'We see both sides of an idea and find interesting things just for the fun of it'* (!)
- *'If you say what if again and again it makes you think again and again and not just stick to one idea'*
- *'It makes you extend your learning'*

A trio of reflections

As we've seen, reflection is an opportunity to stop, think and reassess. It helps all of us to reimagine who we are, what we are doing and how far we have come.

Identify three points in the year when you will give over an extended period of class-time to reflection. Explain to students that in these sessions the purpose is to think about how they are already becoming young people who possess growth mindsets.

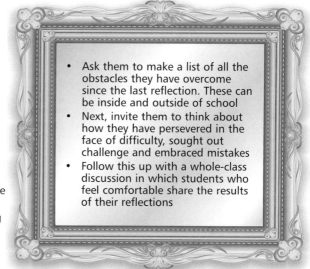

- Ask them to make a list of all the obstacles they have overcome since the last reflection. These can be inside and outside of school
- Next, invite them to think about how they have persevered in the face of difficulty, sought out challenge and embraced mistakes
- Follow this up with a whole-class discussion in which students who feel comfortable share the results of their reflections

Three growth mindset messages

At this stage in the book, let's stop and take stock. Three growth mindset messages are emerging:

1. **The dangers of easy success** (a misguided focus on performance).
2. **The rewards of failure** (a mastery-oriented focus on learning).
3. **The power of meta-learning** (making it all personally meaningful).

Looking for a quick and (ch)easy way of communicating this to your pupils? Try this as a class creed:

> Coming first could be worst
> Coming last may not last
>> But to make my learning even better
>> I need to move on up to meta

To ensure your pupils really 'get it', ask them to explain to a partner exactly what that creed means. Illustrate it. Triple-mount it. Put it to music and choreograph a feral dance. Make it an incantation and recite it daily. Above all, believe it.

Mind Your
Language

It's good to talk

 'The limits of my language mean the limits of my world.'
Ludwig Wittgenstein, philosopher

Wittgenstein taught us that words are tools, not essences – they strain to carry the meaning we wish to communicate. Blunt tools they may be, but they're hugely important tools nonetheless.

In their recent book *Interthinking*, Karen Littleton and Neil Mercer note that thinking creatively and productively together through spoken language is a defining characteristic of our species – and as important today as ever it was. In every classroom, every single day, everywhere in the world, students and teachers talk to each other. What we say has an effect. A big effect. Multiple effects. Drip-drip and big-bang effects. Both ephemeral and unforgettable effects.

This section of the Pocketbook gives you some practical suggestions for harnessing language to influence the development of growth mindsets.

Your story

Think of a time when you were a pupil and someone used the fixed language of judgment, with either positive or negative intent, eg: *'You're the most talented student I've ever taught'*; *'I always thought you were clever'*; *'You'll never amount to much'*.

What were its effects? What did you think and feel when you heard it? How long did these effects last?

Carol Dweck once told Barry that as a doctoral student she was told by her supervisor that she was the ablest student he'd ever had. The result? Immediate gratification and a determination never to put that judgment at risk – so three years of near-silent supervision sessions ensued. Her regret was palpable:

'All those missed opportunities to really talk with and learn from him!'

Fortunately she recovered and went on to develop a growth mindset ...

Tim Martin was once told by a teacher that he'd never be a success in business. He went on to name his pub food chain after this man. You might have heard of J.D. Wetherspoons? Revenge is a dish ...

Your pupils' stories

Tell your story to your class. Be honest about the effects – short and longer term – that it had on you. Now ask them to take five minutes in silence, recalling their own experiences of being judged. Ask them to anonymise the 'judger' but to jot down brief notes under these headings:

What language was used?	
What was its effect?	
Why did it have this effect?	
How do you feel about it now?	

Now ask them to share their stories with a partner. Invite one or two to share their story with the whole class, and then facilitate a discussion around the power of language to do good, and to do harm. Be careful to help draw distinctions between encouragement/ reassurance (which can be empowering/ conducive to growth) and judgment/ labelling (which very rarely is).

A parent's story

Teachers often tell Barry that children get growth mindset messages at school, and fixed mindset messages at home, but that's not always the case. Three years after being introduced to mindset theory this father emailed:

'At home we now bombard our son shamelessly with growth mindset messages. Words such as 'talented', 'intelligent', etc have been removed from our family vocabulary. As a result, Alex* has over time become increasingly self-motivated, hard-working and responsible, but at school and around his friends or extended family he can still get powerful fixed-mindset messages. We went for a parent consultation and his Mum and I still laugh about how many of those fixed-mindset words his teacher managed to fit into the first five minutes of telling us about Alex. He was 'intelligent', 'bright', 'good-natured', 'naturally-this', 'talented at that' ....'

In this instance, it wasn't the parents who were the unwitting villains! The teacher, like (almost) all teachers, is doing her best. With an insight into the effects of mindset on behaviour – and the effect of verbal behaviour on mindset – she could be doing so much better.

*Name changed for anonymity

The power of metaphor

The language of education is well stocked with militaristic metaphors: targets, aims, objectives, strategies, drills, exercises, control, inspections, uniforms, even cohorts!

The metaphors we use have the power to influence the way we see our world and behave within it. The dominant terms above are deeply entrenched (ah, there's another one!) and won't disappear overnight, but you do have the power to assert some control over the language of your classroom. Look out for opportunities to challenge terms with fixed overtones and substitute them with growth-associations:

- See 'problems' (to be avoided) as 'puzzles' (a crossword or Sudoku anyone?)
- See difficulties as opportunities
- See intelligence as acquirable, not merely inheritable – so *'She's very able'* becomes *'She's becoming very able'*

Carol Dweck talks about the value of seeing struggles as desirable learning opportunities: 'Darling I'm home – I've had the most fantastic struggle today!'

A policy audit

If your school has embarked on a growth mindset journey, it can be both informative and helpful to do a 'find and replace' exercise on the school's policy documents. Hunt down those words and terms with fixed mindset overtones, and consider alternatives which have connotations of change and growth. The effect can be rapid and dramatic when these linguistic changes to policy statements become part of the school's habitual discourse. A few candidates:

Fixed overtones	Growth overtones
Ability, more able, highly able	Skills, more skilled, highly skilled
Work (something we do – probably reluctantly – for someone else)	Learning (something we choose to do for ourselves)
Gifted and talented (implied genetic providence)	High achieving (possibly as a result of grit and opportunity)
Rewards (heavily behaviourist and weighted towards compliance)	Recognition (warmly affirming but weighted towards learner autonomy)
Results, performance data, outcomes	Learning, learning, learning

Challenging language

The Nobel prizewinning mathematician John Nash once said that the best way to engage students is simply to ask them the questions that make them think. (Even better, perhaps, is to get *them* to ask the questions – as in P4C.) Your language can challenge students or it can let them off the hook. It can push them to think harder and encourage them to make learning-rich mistakes, or it can do the opposite.

Get your pupils to grow, refine and secure their neural pathways by habitually asking them difficult questions:

- *'Why do you think that? Where's your evidence?'*
- *'How does this fit with what we were saying earlier?'*
- *'How would you try to discover if that is true or not?'*
- *'What are the implications/consequences of this?'*
- *'What do you predict will happen, based on what we know?'*

Build up a repertoire and keep drawing from it.

The hidden persuaders

In 1957 the American journalist Vance Packard released his book *The Hidden Persuaders*. It was about advertising and the techniques advertisers were using to try to sell products. We know that advertising is effective. Great adverts stay with us. Many brands are made famous by the language of their sales pitch:

- 'Just do it'
- 'Every little helps'
- 'It does what it says on the tin'
- 'Never knowingly undersold'

Turn this to your advantage by inviting students to work in groups to create growth mindset advertising campaigns. Give them criteria to meet and ask them to think carefully about the language they use. Conclude by asking groups to present their campaigns to one another.

"Just grow it"

Dramatic confrontation

Drama is a powerful tool in the classroom. It can help pupils to confront fixed mindset voices and dispel the negative emotions they bring. It often draws heavily on a creative use of language. Here's a technique you might like to try:

> Divide your class into groups of three and ask them to imagine they've been invited onto a show called *'Changing the Lives of Fixed Mindsets.'* Indicate that one pupil will play the host, one will play a person who articulates the problems fixed mindsets bring, and one will play a character who knows how to help people change the way they think.
>
> Give pupils time to develop these roles and to come up with ideas they can use in their role-plays. Next, ask them to practise and develop their performances. Finally, invite groups to pair up and take it in turns to show each other their plays. Lead a reflective discussion at the end of the performances.

Getting into role – characters

How does someone with a growth mindset speak? And for that matter, how do they act? These are important questions. We need to know the answers so we can tell when we have successfully taken on the mantle ourselves. Here's another drama-based way to help your students get to grips with these issues:

> Divide the class into groups of four. Give each group a set of four character cards, two of which should describe characters with fixed mindsets, and two should describe characters with growth mindsets. Give students a scenario and ask them to act out their roles (examples on next page). Encourage them to pay special attention to the language they use. Finish by leading the class in a discussion about the language associated with a growth mindset, what this means and why it is important.

Getting into role – scenarios and language bank

Scenarios:

1) Students are discussing the feedback from their latest piece of work.
2) Students are talking about an upcoming test.
3) Students are discussing what makes someone successful.

Language bank:

Growth Mindsets	Fixed Mindsets
'I like learning from my mistakes'	*'I try to avoid mistakes at all costs'*
'The more effort I put in, the better'	*'When things get tough, what's the point?'*
'Being challenged is exciting'	*'It feels uncomfortable when things are hard'*
'You can control your own learning'	*'I don't really think about my learning'*

A guide to guide me

Guides are brilliant! They help us become experts in next to no time. But what about the people who write the guides? They must be experts already. Or, at the very least, they must have had to research the topic and think carefully about it.

So why not take this fact and use it to help your students improve their growth mindset vocabulary? As your pupils become more familiar with the kinds of things outlined in this book, divide the class into groups and invite each group to write a guide on a different area of growth mindset theory and practice. You could start with

MISTAKES
TARGETS
FEEDBACK
LEARNING

Mindset bingo!

This is a classroom game which will get students thinking carefully about the language of growth mindsets.

Begin by asking pupils to draw a 3 x 3 grid on a blank sheet of paper. Next, present them with the following list of words: effort, challenge, perseverance, thinking, learning, feedback, meta-cognition, mind, decisions, growth, fixed, mindset, mistakes, failure, trial and error, stories, reflection, change.

Ask them to select nine of the words to write in their grid. Next, begin reading out definitions of the words. Students cross off their boxes as they hear a definition which matches one of their words. The first pupil to cross off all their boxes shouts out 'Bingo!' Check they are correct in their assumption. As an extension exercise, ask them to generate their own growth mindset words and definitions.

As a rule, mindset activities that are based on children working cooperatively in groups are an excellent way of creating a group growth mindset – the focus of our final chapter.

Growing a Group
Growth Mindset

Growth mindset dispositions

For well over a decade Barry has introduced *mindset* to teachers and pupils with a simple activity. He asks them to reflect on a personal goal or ambition they've achieved in their lives to date, and then to capture the 'how' of their achievement in a single word or phrase. This is the story of their 'hows':

Overwhelmingly popular explanations

Effort

Support from others

Perseverance

Determination

Risk-taking

Having a go

Enjoying the process

Patience

Coping with obstacles

Practice

Planning

Persistence

Making a strategy

Encouragement

Self-belief

Positive self-talk

Trying a different approach

Thinking about times I've achieved difficult things before

Advice

Bounce-back-ability

Interest in it

Imagining myself doing it

Working to repay others' faith in me

Proving others wrong

Constructive feedback

Modifying my goals

Breaking it down into small steps

Having a vision

Sacrifice

Self-discipline

Growth mindset dispositions

Occasional explanations

Luck   Chance   Faith   Realism   Cheating

Rare explanations

Natural ability   Intelligence   Aptitude   A gift or talent

Manipulation   Tubeless tyres   Surgery

It is possible – and usual – to see the popular explanations for achievement as amounting to a 'growth mindset curriculum'. You could use them in just this way. Emphasise the relative value of largely non-cognitive dispositions when compared with the largely cognitive factors identified in the 'rare explanations' category.

Collective mindsets

> '*The way a team plays as a whole determines its success.*'
> **Babe Ruth, baseball legend**

Carol Dweck's research focuses mainly on the effects of particular mindsets on individuals, and that's what we've been looking at in the Pocketbook so far. In this final section of the book we'll be considering the social element in mindset and the value of working to create a collective or group growth mindset.

In Barry's action research with teachers aiming to create growth mindsets in their classes, evidence is emerging that it's not just the mindsets of individual pupils that can change, but those of whole classes and schools too. This is no surprise given that teachers generally set out to support and create growth mindsets in *all* their students, rather than targeting their interventions at particular pupils. Change can be catalytic when groups are working towards the same ends, with exciting possibilities for a 'mindset multiplier effect'.

Cooperative learning groups

It's important to draw a distinction between traditional 'groupwork' (some children in each group doing the work?) and genuinely cooperative groupwork. In their extensive research, Johnson & Johnson found that by far the most impressive learning gains lay with cooperative groupwork. The associations with growth mindset are apparent – it's the learner who takes responsibility for actively growing their skills:

Traditional groupwork	Cooperative groupwork
Minimal interdependence	Active interdependence
Limited individual accountability	Significant individual accountability
One leader (appointed or emergent)	Distributed leadership
Emphasis on task (product)	Emphasis on task *and* relationships
Social skills assumed or ignored	Social skills directly taught
Directive teacher role	Facilitative teacher role
Limited group review/ meta-cognitive reflection	Significant group review /meta-cognitive reflection

Learning together and alone: Cooperative, Competitive and Individualistic Learning D.W Johnson, & R.T Johnson. Pearson, 1999

The link between growth mindset and thinking skills

If you've got some experience of using thinking skills approaches in your class, then you'll immediately recognise the characteristics of cooperative groupwork identified on the previous page.

In well-structured thinking skills tasks *dialogue* (a fluid process associated with learning) – rather than individual brilliance or *knowledge* (crystallised products associated with performance) – is at a premium, and ideas are exchanged, explored and refined between participants. In the process, new knowledge is created and strong inter-personal connections and understandings can be formed as pupils come to see the value of learning with and through others – in a community of learners.

Little wonder that one of the most powerful and transformational of all thinking skills approaches, Philosophy for Children (P4C), is often known as *Community* of Enquiry.

Other thinking skills approaches

In addition to P4C, examples of other thinking skills approaches that can support the development of both individual and group growth mindsets include:

- Dilemma-Based Learning (DBL)
- Logo-Visual Thinking (LVT)
- Thinking Actively in a Social Context (TASC)
- 'Mysteries' and other activities from Thinking Through Geography
- Cognitive Acceleration through Science Education (CASE) and its offshoots in other curriculum areas

A quick online search will reveal books, guides and training opportunities for all these approaches. Each approach has its own unique features, but all are saturated with high-challenge and carefully-calibrated open-ended tasks. They all value effort and challenge; meta-cognition and meta-learning; richness of language use; a toleration of error and failure. And what's more, they all require learners to work with others. As the great educator Lawrence Stenhouse taught us,

 Though children can think *for* themselves, they can't think as well *by* themselves.

Mindset mentors

The regular use of cooperative groupwork activities associated with the thinking skills tradition is one way of encouraging the adoption of a group growth mindset. Another is to deliberately set up social encounters in which pupils can peer-tutor each other in the skills, values and dispositions of growth mindsets.

Carr Manor School in Leeds has an official mindset mentoring system, and the designated 'mindset mentors' are pupils whose role is to support their classmates in developing the dispositions characteristic of growth mindsets.

There are frequent opportunities for pupils and staff to talk publicly about times when they have needed to dig deep and summon up reserves of grit, tenacity, gumption, hope etc. – growth mindsets in action, and celebrated accordingly.

Creating role models

A good mentor acts as a role model. We look up to role models in society and in smaller groups. These people personify the things we think are valuable or important. In your classroom you can make the decision that those students who personify growth mindsets will be your class role models.

Every month, instead of giving out awards, appoint growth mindset role models. You can choose three students, one for each of these (example) categories:

- Effort
- Not being afraid to make mistakes
- Self-regulation (you don't have to simplify the language, but do make sure your pupils know the meanings of the terms)

Change the categories over time and don't fall into the trap of making the appointment too easy to achieve. All must not have mindset prizes! Remember you're not rewarding achievement or ability here, so anyone *could* earn the appointment – but they must work hard for it! It is possible for a group to be appointed if they've demonstrated the category together.

Mindset heroes

To extend and deepen the role model exercise over time, make it *your pupils'* job to:

1. Select and justify the growth mindset qualities that will be valued and looked for.
2. Identify a 'mindset hero' in the public eye who exemplifies these qualities.
3. Nominate, discuss and vote for the classmate who best exemplifies the qualities.

Now construct and display a Weekly (or monthly) Mindset Heroes chart like the one illustrated on the next page.

To provide added power, you could display photos of the global and local hero alongside one another, reinforcing the fact that growth mindset qualities are evidenced globally *and* locally. From little acorns…

Our mindset heroes

Weekly Mindset Hero

Week	Quality	Global hero	Local hero	Reason
1	Resilience (or 'bouncebackability')	Katherine Grainger	Robbie	Robbie did very poorly on his maths test last week but bounced back to work even harder this week
2	Persistence (or grit or 'stick-to-it-iveness')	Ellen MacArthur	Malik	Malik really struggled with his art project but he stuck to it and showed great persistence
3	Openness to criticism	Pope Francis	Miriam	Miriam's views were strongly challenged in our P4C enquiry, but she thought it all through and accepted that her views didn't have a strong evidence base

Teaching the rest of the school

When you teach something, you tend to conflate the subject you are teaching with your own identity. So a maths teacher might see herself as 'someone who knows about and understands maths'. Use this phenomenon to develop a whole school group growth mindset by calling on pupils' knowledge of and expertise in mindset theory.

Challenge your class to create an assembly they can give to the school, their college, house or year group. Explain that the aim is to teach others about growth mindsets – how they work, what they involve and why they are good. Everyone must be involved, whether speaking on stage, preparing research, writing lines or organising costumes.

A less daunting version is to ask pupils to teach other classes in the school. Working in groups of three or four, they create short, interactive presentations about the nature and benefits of growth mindsets. Halfway through the task, groups team up and share ideas. (This encourages a feeling of camaraderie and shared endeavour.) Once they have prepared their teaching materials, groups get together again and identify positive elements of each other's work. Each group then goes off to teach a different class.

Harnessing computers

If your school has a managed learning environment, such as *Frog* or *Fronter*, you can use this to develop your class's growth mindset. Set up a forum and begin a new discussion each week on a different aspect of growth mindsets. Ask your students to contribute at least one post to each discussion and then lead the class in a group conversation about what people have posted the previous week.

Examples of discussion topics include:

- What can we do as a class to develop our mindsets?
- How have you put your growth mindset into action during the last week?
- What are good ways to deal with challenges?
- How might we decide if we have put enough effort into our work?
- What makes a growth mindset?

A mindset wall display

Wall displays can be a powerful means by which to develop group identity.
They offer the possibility for everyone in the class to contribute an individual piece of work which goes on to constitute an important part of the whole. Furthermore, displays remain on the wall for a long time, acting as a constant reminder of the group's emerging identity.

Give each student in your class a sheet of A4 paper and explain that you would like them to divide it in half and to fill in one half with a design which shows them putting the attributes of a growth mindset into action.

When they have done this, ask them to pass their work on one place in a clockwork direction. Students should now create a second design on the blank space which forms half of their new sheet of paper. When everyone has finished, collect in the work and use it to create a 'group growth mindset collage' on one of your display boards.

Using peer-assessment to build group identity

Peer-assessment is any activity in which students give feedback to each other about the work they have created, the skills they have used or the things they have done. By using peer-assessment on a regular basis, you will be able to create a group identity in which learning, support and collaboration are highly valued.

You can develop peer-assessment in your classroom further by training students to focus on the elements which distinguish growth mindsets when they are evaluating the work of their peers.

For example, you might ask pupils to pay close attention to how their peers have responded to difficulties, to the amount of effort they have put in and to the way in which they have learned from their mistakes.

Last words

Growth mindsets increase people's life chances. We see this in their behaviour and in the values that guide it. Here's how a Y6 pupil from Chew Stoke Primary tells it:

> Each day is another step on the staircase of life… Sometimes it seems like we'll never reach the next step… but we move on – we move up. We can soar like birds, struggling against whatever life throws at us; ambition is our wings, carrying us through, making us determined to get there and reach our goal. If you believe you can do it then you can.

We hope that you find the suggestions in this book useful and generative of new ideas and intentions in your own classroom. Feel free to adapt and improve our ideas so that they work in your unique school and classroom environment. If you'd like to share any triumphs or disasters with us, please let us know. Developing our own and others' growth mindsets is a lifelong task – and the more people we can share this with, the better. Good luck on your voyage, and if you'd like an optimistic message to take with you we don't think you could improve on Carol Dweck's words:

> *The hallmark of successful individuals is that they love learning, they seek challenges, they value effort, and they persist in the face of obstacles.*

About the authors

Barry Hymer is Professor of Psychology in Education at the University of Cumbria, Lancaster, where he researches talent development and classroom applications of mindset theory, primarily through school-based practitioner research. He has worked closely with Professor Carol Dweck on two recent European conference tours, with a third in preparation. Recently authored, co-authored and co-edited books include *Dilemma Based Learning in Primary School, The P4C Pocketbook, The Routledge International Companion to Gifted Education, Gifts, Talents and Education: A Living Theory Approach,* and the *Gifted & Talented Pocketbook.* Barry.Hymer@cumbria.ac.uk

Mike Gershon is a teacher, trainer, writer and consultant. He is the author of eight other books on teaching and learning, including *How to use Assessment for Learning in the Classroom, How to use Differentiation in the Classroom,* and *How to use Questioning in the Classroom.* Mike is also the creator of some of the world's most popular online teaching and learning tools; his resources have been viewed and downloaded more than 2.4 million times by teachers in over 180 countries. He also writes regularly on pedagogy for the Times Educational Supplement. Find out more and get in touch at www.mikegershon.com

References and recommended reading

Being Wrong – Adventures in the margin of error
by K. Schultz. Portobello Books Ltd, 2011

Bounce – The Myth of Talent and the Power of Practice
by Matthew Syed. Fourth Estate, 2011

Classrooms as Learning Communities: What's in it for Schools?
by C. Watkins. Routledge, 2005

Creating Learning Without Limits
by M. Swann, et al. Open University Press, 2012

Development of Professional Expertise
by K.A. Ericsson. Cambridge University Press, 2009

Gifted & Talented Pocketbook
by B. Hymer. Teachers' Pocketbooks, 2009

Learning Without Limits
by S. Hart, et al. Open University Press, 2004

Mindset: How You Can Fulfil Your Potential
by Carol Dweck. Robinson, 2012

P4C Pocketbook
by B. Hymer & R. Sutcliffe. Teachers' Pocketbooks, 2012

Praise, Motivation and the Child
by G. Robins. Routlege, 2012

Self-Theories – Their role in Motivation, Personality and Development
by Carol Dweck. Psychology Press, 2000

Visible Learning
by John Hattie. Routledge, 2008